AMAZING SCIENCE
AMAZING MATERIALS

Sally Hewitt

Crabtree Publishing Company

www.crabtreebooks.com

Crabtree Publishing Company
www.crabtreebooks.com

Editors: L. Michelle Nielsen, Michael Hodge
Senior Editor: Joyce Bentley
Senior Design Manager: Rosamund Saunders
Designer: Tall Tree

Photo Credits: BE&W Agencja Fotograficzna Sp. z o. o. /Alamy: p. 25; David Sanger Photography/Alamy: p. 20; Corbis: p. 14; Nick Hawkes/Ecoscene/Corbis: p. 13; Tom & Dee Ann McCarthy/Corbis: p. 22; Jean-Paul Pellssier/Reuters/Corbis: p. 26; Jim Zukerman/Corbis: p. 16; Digital Vision: p. 6; Bridgeman Art Library/Getty Images: p. 8; Arvind Garg/Getty Images: p. 24; Getty Images News: p. 7; John Humble/Getty Images: p. 27; Mark Kelley/Getty Images: cover, p. 18; Dorling Kindersley/Getty Images: p. 3, p. 19; Estelle Rancurel/Getty Images: p. 9; Joel Sartore/Getty Images: p. 17; Steve Satushek/Getty Images: p. 23; Titus/Getty Images: p. 15; Nicola Tree/Getty Images: p. 21; Joseph Van Os/Getty Images: p. 11; Wes Walker/Getty Images: p. 12; Photodisc: p. 10.

Activity & illustrations: Shakespeare Squared pp. 28-29.

Cover: A logger cuts down a tree in Alaska's Tongass National Forest.

Title page: These birds were made by folding sheets of paper.

Library and Archives Canada Cataloguing in Publication

Hewitt, Sally, 1949-
   Amazing materials / Sally Hewitt.

(Amazing science)
Includes index.
ISBN 978-0-7787-3613-4 (bound)
ISBN 978-0-7787-3627-1 (pbk.)

   1. Matter--Properties--Juvenile literature. I. Title.
II. Series: Hewitt, Sally, 1949- . Amazing science.

QC173.36.H49 2007   j530   C2007-904312-7

Library of Congress Cataloging-in-Publication Data

Hewitt, Sally, 1949-
   Amazing materials / Sally Hewitt.
     p. cm. -- (Amazing science)
Includes index.
   ISBN-13: 978-0-7787-3613-4 (rlb)
   ISBN-10: 0-7787-3613-X (rlb)
   ISBN-13: 978-0-7787-3627-1 (pb)
   ISBN-10: 0-7787-3627-X (pb)
   1. Matter--Properties--Juvenile literature. I. Title. II. Series.

QC173.36.H49 2008
530--dc22

                       2007027427

Crabtree Publishing Company
www.crabtreebooks.com   1-800-387-7650

Published in Canada
Crabtree Publishing
616 Welland Ave.
St. Catharines, Ontario
L2M 5V6

Published in the United States
Crabtree Publishing
PMB16A
350 Fifth Ave., Suite 3308
New York, NY 10118

Published by CRABTREE PUBLISHING COMPANY
Copyright © **2008**

Contents

Amazing materials

The Golden Gate Bridge in San Francisco is **made** of steel and concrete. It can stand firm in strong winds and earthquakes.

Steel and concrete are types of **materials**. Materials are what things are made of.

Bricks, **plastic**, **glass**, and **metal** are some materials used every day to build homes, **containers**, cars, and other objects.

The walls of this house are made of bricks.

YOUR TURN!

Collect small things such as pencils, toys, buttons and coins. Find out what materials they are made of.

What is a solid?

This statue is made of a strong, **solid** stone called marble. It looks almost new, but it is nearly 2,000 years old!

Solid materials, such as marble, have **shapes** of their own.

Solid materials are used to make many things. A chair is solid, and so is a book. People are also solid.

A solid chair holds its shape when a person sits on it.

YOUR TURN!

Put some solid objects in a bag. Try to guess what the objects are just by feeling their shapes.

SCIENCE WORDS: solid shape

What is a liquid?

A huge amount of water pours over Niagara Falls every second. Water is always moving and changing shape.

Some materials, such as water, are **liquids**. Liquids take on the shape of the containers that they are in.

A liquid does not have a shape of its own.

YOUR TURN!

Collect jugs, mugs, and bottles. Pour water from one to the other. Watch the water take the shape of the container.

Water can also be solid. It can freeze into ice.

SCIENCE WORDS: **liquid   container**

What is a gas?

Hot **air** fills a balloon and lifts it high into the sky. The hot air takes the shape of the balloon.

Air is a kind of **gas**. A gas is a material that moves and changes shape. Gases are not as **dense** as liquids are.

You cannot see air, but it is all around you. You need air to live.

Smoke is a kind of gas. It changes shape as it moves.

YOUR TURN!

Your breath is a kind of gas. Blow up a balloon. Watch your breath take the shape of the balloon.

SCIENCE WORDS: **gas air**

Changing shape

A potter shapes a lump of clay into a pot. The soft, wet clay is baked hard in a kiln, or special oven.

Some materials can be squashed and stretched into different shapes.

You can squash, stretch, and change the shape of soft dough. Dough **hardens** when it is baked and becomes breads or cakes.

Cutting bread changes its shape.

YOUR TURN!

Change the shape of clay by making a pot or sculpture. Watch the clay harden as it dries.

SCIENCE WORDS: soft hard change

Melting and molding

Dump trucks and cranes are **molded** from metal. Metal is a strong material that is used to make machines than can handle tough jobs.

Metal is found in rocks. Iron and gold are kinds of metal.

Very hot metal **melts** and becomes a liquid. It is poured into a container called a "mold".

When some liquid metals cool, they harden into solid that are the shape of the mould.

YOUR TURN!

Ask an adult to help you make jelly. When liquid jelly cools, it takes on the shape of the jelly mold.

SCIENCE WORDS: **melt   metal   mold**

Wood and paper

A huge tree can take hundreds of years to grow. Trees are often cut down for their wood.

Wood is a **natural** material. It can be cut with tools to make objects such as chairs and pencils.

Wood can be chopped into small pieces, mixed with water, and pressed to make paper.

YOUR TURN!

It is easy to change the shape of paper. Fold a piece of paper into a paper airplane. Throw it and watch it fly.

You can fold, cut, and write on paper.

SCIENCE WORDS: cut fold

Glass

This chandelier is made of sparkling glass. Glass was once dry sand. It is a hard material, but it breaks easily.

Sand is heated with other materials to make glass.

Light shines through glass. It is transparent, which means that you can see through it.

Windows are made of flat sheets of glass.

YOUR TURN!

Find things that are made of glass. Why do you think they are made of glass?

SCIENCE WORDS: **glass   transparent**

Plastic

A small child can pick up a big toy fire engine. The fire engine is light because it is made of plastic.

Plastic is a material made in a factory. It can be molded into all kinds of shapes.

Water does not soak through plastic because it is a **waterproof** material.

YOUR TURN!

Pour water on different materials. Which materials are waterproof?

A plastic coat, boots, and an umbrella keep you dry in the rain.

Cloth

Silk is a material that is often used to make clothing, such as **saris**. Silk threads are made by silk worms. The threads are then woven into silk **cloth**.

Silk, **cotton**, and **wool** are natural materials. Cotton comes from plants, and wool comes from sheep.

Cloth made from silk, cotton, wool, and other materials is cut and sewn to make clothes.

A teddy bear is made of soft cloth. A toy car is made of tough plastic.

YOUR TURN!

Collect pieces of cloth. Cut them into shapes, and glue them onto cardboard to make a picture or pattern.

SCIENCE WORDS: silk wool cotton

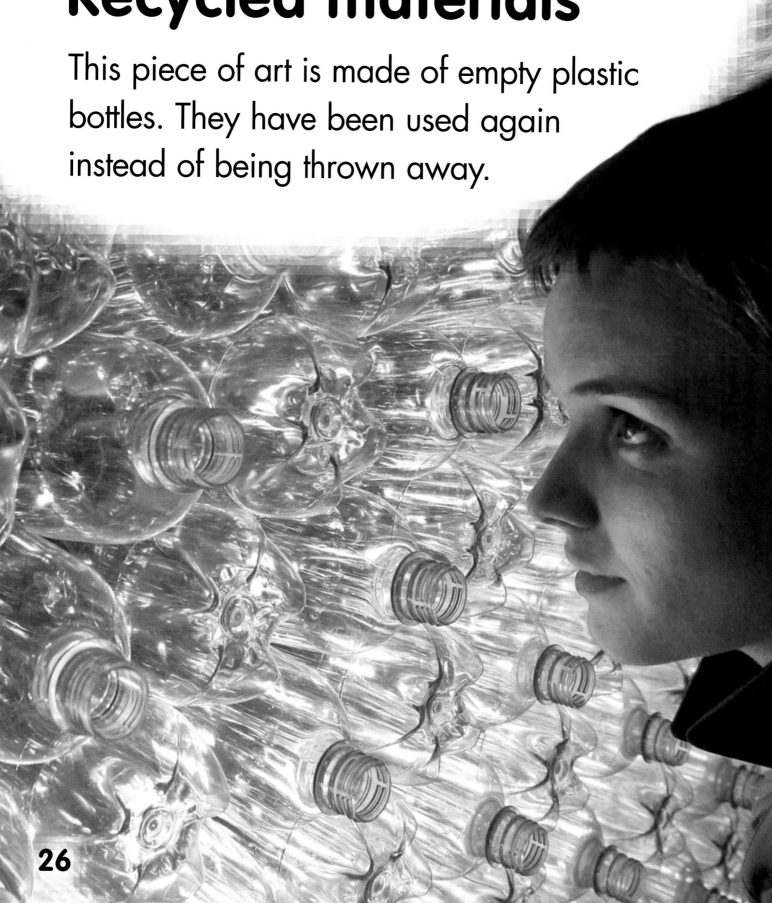

Recycled materials

This piece of art is made of empty plastic bottles. They have been used again instead of being thrown away.

Using materials over again is called "recycling".

Plastic, paper, and metal are materials that can be recycled and made into something new.

Waste paper can be recycled to make more paper.

YOUR TURN!

Do not **waste** *materials. Recycle paper, plastic, and cans instead of throwing them away.*

SCIENCE WORDS: recycled   waste

An airy experiment

Air is all around us, but does it take up space? Complete this activity to see whether air takes up space like other materials.

What you need
- large 2 qt. (1.9 L) clear bowl
- small piece of cork
- water
- clear plastic cup

1. Fill the large bowl about three-quarters of the way full with water. Make sure that you add at least this much water. If there is not enough water, it will be difficult to see the results.

2. Place the cork in the bowl of water. The cork should float on the surface of the water. Try to make sure that the cork is in the center of the bowl.

3. Hold the open end of the plastic cup just above the piece of cork. Make sure that the cork is not touching any part of the cup.

4. Press the open end of the cup over the cork and into the water. Press the cup all the way down to the bottom of the bowl. What has happened?

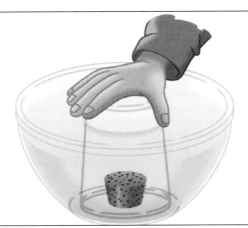

What happened:

The air that we breathe is a gas. Gas takes up space, just like a solid or liquid material does. When you push the cup down into the water, the piece of cork is forced to the bottom. How can this happen if the cork floats? When you push the cup down, you trap a pocket of air inside it. There is no place for the water to go. The air in the cup forces the water and the cork to the bottom of the bowl. Although we cannot see most gases, they do take up space just like the water in the bowl and the bowl itself.

Glossary

air A gas that is all around us that we cannot see.

cloth Cloth is a material that is made by weaving or knitting threads together.

container A box, bottle, or jug that is used to hold things.

cotton The fibers of some plants that are used to make fabrics, or cloths.

dense An obect that is dense has the parts that make it up closely packed together. Objects can be very dense or not dense at all. A solid is denser than a liquid, and a liquid is denser than a gas.

gas A material that moves and changes shape. Air is a kind of gas.

glass A material that you can see through and that breaks easily. Windows are made of glass.

hardens A material that becomes harder. Things that are hard are difficult to cut, bend, or break.

liquid Liquid materials flow and do not have a shape of their own.

made Things that are made are not natural. They are made in a factory or by hand.

materials Materials are what things are made of. Paper, wood, and plastic are materials.

melt   To change something from a solid into a liquid by heating it.

metal   A material found in rock. Iron and gold are kinds of metal.

molded   To make into a shape. Liquid materials are poured into molds and left to harden into the shapes of the molds.

natural   Natural things have not been made by hand or in a factory. They are made by nature.

plastic   Plastic is not a natural material. It is made in a factory.

recycled   Things that are recycled have been used again.

saris   Silk clothing worn mainly by women from India and Pakistan.

shape   The outline of something.

silk   A fine cloth of silk threads. Silk threads are made by silkworms.

soft   Soft things feel smooth and are easily squashed or bent.

solid   Things that are solid have their own shapes.

waste   You waste something when you throw it away instead of using it again.

waterproof   Waterproof material keeps out water. Raincoats are made of waterproof material.

wool   A material made from the woolly coat of a sheep.

Index

Printed in the USA